Copyright © 2023 Javier Negrete
All rights reserved.
ISBN: 9798390049174

Dedication

To my beloved Kermit,
the happiest and most adventurous orange cat I know. On this special day, we celebrate not just another birthday, but the joy, laughter, and love you have brought into my life. Your boundless energy, curiosity, and affection have made my days brighter and my heart warmer. May this birthday be filled with all the things that make you smile - a loving family, loyal friends, and memories that will last a lifetime. Happy Birthday, Kermit! May you continue to chase the sun, climb the tallest trees, and never lose your zest for life.

With love and happiness,
Javie

This book belongs to:

_____

In a cozy little house
at the end of the street,
Lived a birthday cat
named Kermit, so sweet.

His whiskers were twitching,
his tail swished with glee,
For his birthday was coming,
as special as can be!

His dad was excited, planning the day,
Making sure everything was perfect in every way.

Invitations were sent to friends far and wide,
To come and join Kermit and celebrate by his side.

There was Haku the cat,
and Nelo the hound,
And Nova the kitten
who'd surely be around.

On the morning of the party, Kermit awoke with a smile, Knowing his friends would be there in just a short while.

Balloons of all colors
and a cake so divine,
Dad had prepared everything,
right down the line.

The party games started,
with chase and hide-and-seek,
The animals laughed and played,
their joy at its peak.

There was a piñata shaped like a fish,
Bursting with treats that all guests would relish.

Dad lit the candles on Kermit's cake with a flare, And everyone gathered around, their eyes full of care.

Kermit closed his eyes, and with all of his might, He wished for more days filled with love and delight.

As he blew out the candles,
the room filled with applause,
Everyone knew that this
was the best of all paws.

Gifts were unwrapped, and treats were all shared,
And the happiness in the room simply couldn't be compared.

As the sun began to set,
and the party drew to an end,
Kermit hugged his friends tightly,
grateful for each special friend.

THE END

To Kermit, our dear feline friend, On this special day, our love we send. A birthday filled with joy and cheer, A celebration for all to hear.

Oh, Kermit, you're a ray of sun, Your boundless energy, second to none. In your presence, the world's aglow, A vibrant orange, head to toe.

With whiskers twitching, tail held high, You leap and bound, reaching for the sky. An orange comet, swift and bright, A furry wonder, pure delight.

On this birthday, we gather 'round, With friends and family, love is found. A day of laughter, cake, and fun, For you, dear Kermit, our cherished one.

Happy Birthday, to our dear cat, The one, the only, the orange diplomat. May your future hold endless glee, Forever happy, wild, and free.

Printed in Great Britain
by Amazon